LELA GIBSON

Freedom

How To Make Money Online And Become Financially Free By Creating Passive Income

LELA GIBSON

LELA GIBSON

CONTENTS

LELA GIBSON

Introduction

I want to thank you and congratulate you for buying the book, "Freedom: How to Make Money Online and Become Financially Free by Creating Passive Income".

This book has lots of actionable information that you can use to make money online and become financially free by creating passive income.

Do you know the sweetest thing in the world? Well, one word; freedom! More precisely, the freedom from the confines of a 9-5 job! Unfortunately, freedom is not easy to come by since we live in a currency driven world where financial freedom is a fickle mistress. Even so, the best way to create financial freedom is by starting a business that earns you a passive income.

With the advancement of technology, anyone can invest online and start generating, hundreds, thousands and even millions of dollars. However, the success of your online business depends on some things such as your business idea and your business managerial prowess.

If you are ready to start an online business but are unsure of where to start or how to go about it, do not worry; this passive income guide will equip you with valuable knowledge guaranteed to help you start an online business that earns you a passive income.

Thanks again for buying this book. I hope you enjoy it!

Before you can learn the specifics of building a passive income, it is critical that you understand what you are venturing into so that you don't start with a wrong idea of what it is you are working towards as well as what to expect from your efforts. Let's begin.

Passive Income: A Comprehensive Background

Passive income, also called residual income is simply the money you earn when you are not actively working. If you are actively working, it means you will receive some money (active income), which, when you stop working, you stop earning.

With contract work or active work, you have to do some work to receive pay. In other words, you MUST exchange your time (hours, minutes, days, weeks or even months) for pay. In that case, if you are not working, you cannot be paid; it is simple logic!

This is always not the case with passive income. With passive incomes, you earn whether you work actively or not. To create a passive income stream, you will have to put in some work upfront to get the ball rolling. You will however get to a point where your income stream will become passive such that it generates revenue on its own without you having to work for it.

Think of publishing a book on Amazon for instance. After doing the upfront work of writing and promoting the book in its initial stages, you will get to a point whereby the book can continue making money whether you do anything to promote it or not. That's passive income!

Before we head any further, we have to discuss some things about passive income because these things are important and will help you understand the nature of a passive income. Some of these include:

1: Passive incomes are often not permanent incomes: Get it right: some online passive incomes may last for years, decades, or even centuries. They can however never be permanent. This is because all forms of income eventually dry up at a given point for one reason or another.

Going with the example of publishing an Amazon book, after you write the book, publish, and promote it, you can sit back as passive income dollars or pounds stream into your bank account. However, because even the best books are not perpetually evergreen, a time will come when your "once bestselling book" shall slip off the ranks to a rank where it earns very little if any.

How long a passive income stream lasts depends on the idea itself, more specifically, the popularity of the idea, the implementation plan how well you execute the idea and the quality of your investment.

2: *It is not a one-time lump sum payment:* Some incomes such as inheritance, sale of assets like pieces of land, or sale of stocks are one-time lump sum payments. This is not the case with passive income since passive income is a source of income that has a sense of continuity over a certain period.

As an example, if you invest in Amazon publishing whereby you create and publish several books, you will earn royalties on these books. Amazon shall send the royalties to you on a monthly basis at a designated time. The same applies to other passive income strategies.

For instance, if you create a blog and monetize it through affiliate marketing, the monies you earn from your affiliate recommendations will not be lump sum payments. The payments will be continuous and will vary from month to month depending on the vibrancy of your affiliation.

3: *Some passive incomes are semi-passive:* You may be your own boss but you will need to do some work (even if its management), although you will not receive pay for maintaining your investment.

For instance, if you build a house and rent it out, you will definitely receive your passive income from the tenants but when they move out, you will have to invest some energy, money, and time to maintain the vacated premise and seek other tenants. The same applies to online passive income streams.

For instance, if you create a product and sell it online, while you will never have to create the same product again, you will have to engage in the marketing of the product even if your participation in the process is as little as directing the marketing team. The other thing is that even in such an instance, you will have to play an active or semi-active role in the management of the business.

Another more succinct example is that of blogging. When you start a monetized blog, you will have to create blog posts (or find the correct person to do it), manage the blog, find affiliate offers that match your blogging niche, or even do other things such as prospects for back links and promote the blog and affiliate offers.

Therefore, most passive income streams are semi-passive in nature when you take into account the work required to maintain them.

4: *Passive income streams need maintenance:* Whether it is checking emails or paying taxes on your passive income, you have to do some of these activities for maintenance since they keep your source of passive income going.

5: *Your passive income might be another person's active Income:* No matter what kind of online business you invest in, you will have to hire people to do some work that help you earn your passive income. In other words, your passive income builds on leveraging on other people's active income to succeed! For example, if you have a freelance writing marketplace for instance, you will have to hire some people who will be writing or editing your articles. You will have to pay them hence they will receive active income but their work is what shall help you earn a passive income.

Now that we have established these critical things about passive income streams, the next thing we have to consider is why the internet is the best way to create multiple passive income streams.

Why The Internet: The Internet As A Way To Earn Passive Income

Online investments are a true deal. If you are doubtful of this, just look at Mark Zuckerberg, the creator of Facebook. Can you guess his worth? He is worth about $53.5 billion and his worth is rapidly increasing daily. Do you know what perhaps makes Facebook, which has been in business for slightly over 13 years (founded in 2004) such a huge success? Well, because it is deployed on a massive scale through the internet; all that the employees at Facebook need to do is to keep the system functional (system in this case is website, servers, new functionalities etc.) and the rest is income being made on autopilot. No one goes to a Facebook offline shop to make a payment- everything is done automatically! Well, you don't have to create the next Facebook; the point I am making here is that once deployed, the earning potential is literally limitless!

Another online source of passive income is music. Look at Justin Bieber, a teen pop singer whose career started through YouTube; over the last 2 years, Bieber has earned more than $108 million.

Karmin is another pop duo who signed a million dollar deal with Chris Brown after their cover of the original "Look at Me Now" went viral and generated more than 100 million views.

When it comes to blogs and websites, look at John Wu, the founder of Bankaholic.com website. In 2008, he managed to sell his website for $14.9 million. That's not all; in 2010, Michael Arrington sold his Entrepreneurial tech blog site TechCrunch to AOL for a staggering $30 million.

We cannot forget to mention fashion bloggers such as Leandra Medine. Medine founded the Man Repeller blog. Her website grew so popular that it gave birth to two jewelry lines (collaboration with Dannijo and Del Toro), earning her $325, 000.

Sophia Amoruso, the founder of Nasty Gal online clothing store started by selling vintage items on eBay, a project that built her fan-base and upon outgrowing her platform, she started her own clothing store. Today, the Nasty Gal clothing store is worth $130 million.

Authors earn a passive income too. For example, Louise Ross, the author of the romance thriller 'Holy Island' sold more than 100, 000 copies (online) in less than a year. This book earned her about $1 million despite even after rejection from a number of publishers.

Yes, it has happened and it is still happening: thousands of people are using the internet to create passive income streams. What are you waiting for? Your talent or passion might make you the next internet millionaire or even billionaire if you put your mind to it. As they say, it is better to try and fail (which of course you will not because you have this book to guide you and give you the secret to internet business success) than to never try at all.

You may be one of the lucky few who shoot funny or crazy videos and post them on YouTube and within no time, the video has more likes and views than you can imagine. This video might prompt YouTube to get in touch with you asking for partnership. Do you know what that means? YouTube will run ads on your popular channel and share the revenue with you! How cool is that? Well, besides that, you stand to derive many other benefits from building a passive income online.

Other than the above, you also have to consider the massive nature of the internet. Internet penetration records show that the world has over 4 billion active internet users. From a business perspective, no news could be as exciting. Can you imagine how much power this gives you?

Let's do the math. Assume that like John Wu or the other persons above, you create an amazing online business driven by passing income; a business a portion of the 4 billion people online rave about. For instance, say you capture a million of these people and they become raving fans. Can you see the scalability of this? Even if each of these people bought something worth 2 dollars each month, that would be $2 MILLION! That is quite a huge number.

LELA GIBSON

Why You MUST Build An Online Passive Income Stream

Some of the benefits you can get from an online passive income include the following:

You Become Your Own Boss

By having an online business or investment that generates a passive income, you automatically become your own boss. This means you can do whatever you want and plan for your hours without any limitations. This is very dissimilar to an active income stream where your boss will plan for your hours.

When you start a profitable online business, you will be making your own schedule. Imagine working for 3-4 hours and then spending the rest of your time doing other things such as pursuing your hobbies or spending time with your friends or family. This is a very interesting idea, one most people do not get to do.

Lower Taxes

When you start your passive income stream, you will pay fewer taxes because business taxes are lower for online businesses than taxes for active jobs hence, only a small amount of your passive income will go to taxes.

14

Unlimited Income Potential

With active work, no matter how much work you do or how many raises you get, there will always be a ceiling. Your boss will always pay you the agreed amount. In any case, you can only work for so many hours. Even if you climb up the corporate ladder fast, you can bet that if you are exchanging your time for money, your earning potential is limited.

However, with passive income businesses (if set properly), your earning potential is limitless. With all online sources of passive income, you will not have any limitation to the amount you earn. The amount you earn will depend on how well you establish your source of income following the right steps (we shall see these later).

A good example of this is affiliate marketing. When you affiliate your site to one product or service, you can earn from that affiliation. Of note here is that as you create blogs and content for your site, you can insert that link many times and earn from it many times over. You can also insert into the content other links to other referral platforms.

A great example of this is Nick Loper of sidehustle.com. In early 2017, Nick published a blog post that earned him $7620 in addition to what his blog earns him. These earnings came from different affiliate links inserted into the content multiple times. Imagine what you can do with such a system. What if, instead of 1 blog, you had 10, 20, or even 30 such blogs. How much money would that generate on a monthly basis? A lot!

Creativity Freedom

It is your job; you responsible for setting the goals, missions, and visions of your investment. This will allow you the opportunity to think and consult different people for different ideas. Above all, you will always make the final decisions. You will have the freedom to be creative, an opportunity that will motivate you to work towards your set goals. This is unlike most active work where you have to follow a certain method set by your boss or the company you work for.

Location Independence

For most active income streams, you will have a fixed workplace where you will have to report on time every day as agreed. Your fixed work area could be a cubicle your boss gave you as your workstation probably because he wants to track you as you work.

For online passive incomes, no one is there to watch you or track your movements during work hours because you are your own boss and you can do whatever you want. The most important thing in online passive work is a computer, and an access to the internet.

You can carry your personal computer to the beach, to your home, or even in your vehicle, coffee shop, and still work from there. It is up to you to decide whether to have a fixed workplace or not.

Even with its lucrative outlook, passive income has many misconceptions some of which we will debunk next.

Passive Income Misconceptions

Because it is gaining rapid popularity, online passive income streams are generating tons of myths and misconceptions. Let us bust some of the main ones:

You Just Need a Couple of Days to Make Thousands of Dollars Passively Online

If you thought that you would just create an idea such as a video, post it on YouTube, and then after a few days, you wake up with thousands of dollars in your bank account, you are so wrong. It will take months or even years to create a good business out of your idea.

For example, if you want to create something you think your community wants, the first thing you have to do is to lay the groundwork, research what they need, and then figure out how best to give it to them (an activity that could take months or years).

Passive Income is 100% Passive

Whether your project requires maintenance or not, you will have to work even if the only work you do is setting up things at the beginning of your project. No income is 100% passive; if you thought you do not need to work to start or maintain your passive income stream, think again.

Even after your business has a stable base and is earning you great amounts of money, you will still have do work adjacent things such as checking your pages or links in case of breakdowns or update a website theme. For sustainability, you also must know what your customers think about your product, carry out tests to know what works and what doesn't etc.

Having Employees Will Make Your Work Harder

You might want to work alone because you think you will succeed easily. However, the truth is that utilizing teams for your online passive business has many benefits such as:

1. You can be a source of income to other people hence contributing to their success.

2. Your employees can run your business for you hence allowing you time to do other things.

3. By having a team, you will be opening yourself and your business up for more opportunities because they will help you sell your idea.

It Is Easy Money

Many people think generating an online passive income is an easy way to earn money but the truth is; while this may be so, it is not always the case. Every business or investment will need some capital, time, and energy.

You will come across many competitors because you are not the only player in the game. As a result, you will have to work hard to keep up with the competition. You will have to do something more to stay one-step ahead. If you thought you would sleep all day and then find money in your bank account in the evening, it is best to wake up now and start figuring out what you want to do.

Now that we have looked at the benefits of running an online passive income business as well as busted some of the myths surrounding passive income, the next question is; which types of online businesses can you run online to generate passive income for you? That's what we will discuss next.

Online Passive Income Streams

There are many online business ideas you can start today and start earning a passive income. Some of these include:

Make Passive Income Through Blogging

Blogging is increasingly becoming very popular these days thanks to the endless ways it makes the bloggers to derive satisfaction from their readers (through income, engagement etc.). And given that a blog can give you an endless list of ways through which you can make money once you have build a readership (I will show you how), this makes blogs a core part of every successful online business. So how can you go about creating a successful blog? That's what we will discuss next.

How to Start Blogging for Money

To create a revenue generating blog, do the following:

Step 1: Start a Blog

If you want to use blogging to create a passive income stream, you must have a blog. If you do not have one, no worries; here are the steps you should follow to create your blog.

Decide On What to Blog About

The main aim of any blog is to become the recommended resource for its topic of discussion. Before you decide on what to blog about, make sure to choose a topic that you enjoy, a topic with plenty of room for discussion, and most importantly, a topic you can easily establish yourself as an authority.

Choose a Platform

The internet has many services that can help you start a blog (platforms) that may leave you confused without knowing what to go for. Do not go for a free service; you might want to save a dollar or two but remember that investing in a good platform is a determinant of how much you will earn from your blog. WordPress is an inexpensive, flexible, easy to use, and popular platform you can try.

Choose a Domain Name (Web Address)

If you do not have a domain name, you have to come up with one. It might not be hard to come up with a name but coming up with a good, unique name no one owns may be a tad difficult. If you find it hard to come up with your own name, you can visit a platform such as namemesh to generate domain name ideas and then use a domain name registrar such as GoDaddy.com, iPage.com, Hostgator.com, Bluehost.com or NameCheap.com to register your domain.

When it comes to choosing a domain name, you should pay attention to several things. Key among this is the nature of your business and its interest. Here is what this means:

If you choose to create a blog about a topic such as DIY home repair, the name you choose as your domain name should have a relationship, no matter how dismal, with this topic. For instance, you cannot give a DIY home repair blog a name such as doghabits.com or lovequote.com. That would be ludicrous and would only end up misleading potential readers. You want to keep the domain name relevant to your niche. In this example, a domain name such as DIYrepairsjournal.com or easyhomerepairs.com would be ideal.

The other thing worth noting is that the domain name should be easy to remember and even easier to type. This means you should keep it brief; it also means you should avoid numbers and hyphens whenever possible.

The other thing to consider is your chosen domain name prefix. .com and .org are the best; however, do not shy from using a .me if it fits in well with your business.

Choose a Web Host

Finding a good web host will allow other people to find your site on the internet. Many of the free or cheap web hosts available today will tempt you to sign up. However, to be a successful blogger, it is critical that you opt for a self-hosted blog, which is where the need to choose a web host comes in. The thing is; many of the companies that sell domain names also offer web-hosting services. Therefore, feel free to try their service.

When choosing a webhost, pay special attention to several things. The first is your budget; there is no point in choosing a webhost whose monthly payments you cannot manage comfortably. The other thing is the backend support. If you have zero website development skills, it's best to go with a host that offers backend installations such as WordPress installation. Support, i.e. the availability and responsiveness of your chosen host is another important consideration. In the same breath, you should also consider the allowed bandwidth. If you envision a future where your blog becomes so popular that you attract millions of visits per day or month, choose a webhost that will match this future bandwidth.

After you have selected a niche, chosen a domain name and have your blog hosted, you can move on to the next step, which is to set up your blog. Assuming that you are using WordPress.org, you need to install it on your web host; there is usually a one click install button when you have logged in to your control panel; use that to install WordPress. After that, you will need to actually set up the blog to be the way you want it to look like.

As you set up your blog, it is also important to make your blog search engine friendly. You can do that by optimizing your blog for search engines to ensure you generate organic traffic (the traffic that comes to your website after someone types certain keywords on their preferred search engine).

Search engine optimization for blogs does not have to be difficult. In fact, to get started, all you have to do is install the plugin (you do this on your WordPress management dashboard) SEO Yoast. Once installed, this plugin will give you optimization ideas for all the pages and blog posts you create on your blog. It will highlight the areas you need to work on in red and the ok areas in green. This proves very useful because even in an instance where you know zero about search engine optimization, you can still create a search engine friendly blog.

Step 2: Create Content

For your blog to generate a passive income, you have to create useful content on your chosen topic to attract readers. Most readers like blogs that talk about:

Solving problems: We hate feeling frustrated. If you can think of something that frustrates many people and you can post a good solution to it, start writing the solution, and see how you can have many readers.

Reaching a goal: Do you have a goal you once set, reached it (for example getting out of debt or losing weight), and you think many people have the same goal but do not know how to go about achieving it? This is a prime chance to earn a passive income. Simply spell out what you did and how you did it to inspire others in similar situations.

Entertainment: If you lead a wildly interesting life or are outrageously funny, you can create entertainment blogs. The only thing you need is creativity that will help you create a uniquely entertaining story. You can also make your story entertaining and at the same time helpful.

For example, if you keep camels at home and you decide to write an interesting story about camels, do not just mention that you raise them; you can include some information on how you do it. From this, you are likely to attract many readers because your story will be entertaining and helpful.

The thing about content is that readers want quality content that meets their expectations. You MUST strive to fulfill that expectation by publishing high quality blog posts frequently.

As you publish great content, don't forget to start building a readership for your blog.

Are you enjoying this book? Leave a review on Amazon!

Step 3: Build a Social Media Relationship

You may be creating great content but getting very few readers because of a bad social media presence. Be active: participate on social media group discussions, comment on other people's blogs, and find people who could benefit from your blog and be friendly to them. If they find your blog interesting, these people will help you by recommending your blog posts to their social circles.

Always remember to use social media sites where most of your target audience hangs out. For example, if you write an entertainment blog, Facebook, Twitter and Instagram are probably the best sites for you.

Note: As a rule of thumb, make sure every blog post is optimized for sharing on the different platforms and have social sharing buttons at the bottom of every post. You can set up every post for sharing on social platforms by making sure each post has great images, infographic, GIF and other types of images to increase their ease of sharing; people love visually appealing content!

Step 4: Build a Strong Platform

You have to continue researching so that you can improve your craft knowledge and increase your valuable and deep content output and thus create a super strong platform. In addition, it is also important to consider the type of reputation you want to have. How do you want your readers to perceive you? What do you want them to know you for? Brand your name and your work.

Here are some of the things that will help you build a strong platform:

Have a good headshot and consistent avatar: That small photo you attached to your social media sites is very important. Look for a good photographer or take good photo. Attach it where you should attach it and leave it there as your logo. This image will associate with all your work.

Do not change your avatar any time you want because doing so will confuse your readers: Imagine how confusing it would be if a famous company kept changing its logo every week. This is what you do to your readers if you whimsically change your avatar! Choose one avatar you will use across the internet to ensure consistency.

Post carefully and thoughtfully: You definitely have competitors who want to see you fail. To avoid their victory, write and share carefully if you do not want things and stuffs that are private or anonymous coming back to haunt you in the future. You can share something with a friend and within no time, it goes viral, ruining your reputation. So yeah, be careful with what you post online.

Be real: Some bloggers portray themselves as one way online when they are something different in real life. This is a very wrong way of building a platform because one day, your online and offline worlds will collide and you will lose many readers because they will realize you have been dishonest.

To avoid this, make your two worlds congruent. If you have decided to portray a particular quality online, try as much as possible to make it your real life quality.

Step 5: Choose Your Monetization Options

The number of ways through which you can monetize your blog is literally limitless especially because almost all the other methods of making money online can to be backed/supported by a blog or website if they are to succeed.

Here are some ways through which you can monetize your blogs:

Displaying ads: I want you to think of your blog as a TV station and your audience as the viewers; the bigger your audience is, the more the earning potential for advertising. There are different forms of advertising though; direct advertising and using ad networks. With direct advertising, you agree with an individual or company to display ads about their product/service for a given period for a fee. With ad networks however, you register to an ad network then connect your blog to the network so that the network can display relevant ads on your blog to your audience. In this case, if you go for an ad network, you are paid for every click. Some popular ad networks include:

- Google AdSense

- RevContent

- Adsterra

- Ad Maven

- AdRecover

- BlogAds

- Media.Net

- Advertising.com

- Clicksor

- Chitika

- AdCash

- PropellerAds

- InfoLinks

- Adbuff

- AdBlade

- BidVertiser

When starting out, ad networks are the best option for you because they don't have requirements that are too high and the fact that they look for the paying advertisers (customers) so that you can focus on creating great content that keeps your visitors coming back to your blog. The only downside to this method is that you really need a lot of visitors to make any significant amount of money from blogging.

As your blog grows and depending on its nature, you can then start doing sponsored posts i.e. you publish a blog about a certain brand, service or issue of interest to another person for a small fee.

Besides advertising, you can use your blog to make money in other ways including:

- Affiliate marketing

- Selling your own products/services

- Supporting your publishing business

- Having a membership site

- Selling courses

- And much, much more!

We will discuss some of these ways as we go on starting with affiliate marketing.

Make Passive Income Through Affiliation Marketing

This is a passive income stream where your blog acts like a salesperson for selling other people's products online. When someone buys a product through your referral link, you earn a commission. Some products pay as high as 80-90% commissions, especially digital downloadable products. Physical products and services (where active work is involved) typically pay less affiliate commissions (5-20% maybe).

The thing with blogging and earning affiliate income is that when you develop a loyal audience, you can bet that they are likely to want to buy whatever products/services you are recommending, which essentially means your earning potential is high. All you have to do is to post a blog post with a link to the affiliate product, share it on social media and to your mailing list then wait for your affiliate commissions to start streaming in. The larger your loyal audience, the greater your earning potential.

The good thing about affiliate marketing is that there are no investments, no inventory, no product shipping, no fees, and above all, your blog will be around for many years meaning you will end up earning money from a link you posted immediately after your now 5-year old blog.

How to get started With Affiliate Marketing

To get started with affiliate marketing:

If you already have a blog (we learnt how to go about it in the previous chapter), you don't need to create any other website; you can start right away.

Join Affiliate Programs

You can join many of the available affiliate programs; examples include:

Avangate

CJ

ClickBank

Rakuten Affiliate Network

ShareASale

Amazon Associates

JVZoo

eBay Partner Network

MaxBounty

Flex Offers

AvantLink

All you have to do is to join any of the above programs, see how they work and perhaps start promoting products that are relevant to whatever it is you are blogging about, as this makes it easy to promote/recommend products to your current audience. Upon registration, you will receive an affiliate ID and perhaps a unique link for every product that you are promoting to help the company and yourself to track affiliate sales, as well as commissions. Simply figure out how a certain product will make the lives of your audience better when posting a blog post/sending an email to your email subscribers (yes, your blog needs to have an email opt-in form to help you to collect your audience's email addresses so that you can reach out to them later).

Obviously, the above list does not in any way represent all the affiliate programs out there. You can simply search "affiliate networks" on your favorite search engine to display some more.

Some products/service may have affiliate programs not listed on the website. If you love a product and you cannot see its affiliate program on its website, contact the company to see if they have an affiliate program. For most companies, it is free to become an affiliate. If a company is asking you to pay a fee to join its affiliate program, you are staring at a scam. Therefore, always be careful.

So what are your options as far as posting content that helps you to generate leads and perhaps earn you a commission in the end? Let's discuss that next.

Step 3: Link Promotion

There are different ways to promote your affiliate links. They include:

Comparing products: You can decide to write content comparing 2 or several products. This will help your readers make purchase decision by weighing the pros and cons of each product. The thing is; whichever option that people choose, you can stand a chance to earn affiliate commissions in the process. You can compare the products side by side (in a table) or compare them in pros (where you discuss the pros and cons of each).

Creating tutorials: You can decide to document anything that involves a process on YouTube videos. You can also document something already documented if you think you can do it better. By doing so, you will help your readers save time and money (since they will not have to watch all over for tutorials before they settle for the one they are looking for) and as a result, you will end up having many readers. With this approach, you can place your affiliate link on the video description.

Always mention the product in your content: This is an easy way to promote your link because all you will have to do is mention the product and hyperlink it. For example, if you are writing an article on how to cook pancakes, you can provide a link to where you buy certain ingredients for instance.

Product reviews: If you decide to write an in depth product review, all you need to do is provide your honest review of the product. If you write a glowing review for a bad product thinking you will earn an affiliate income, you are in for a rude shock. When your product reviews are honest, your readers will reward you (for loyalty) and above all, they will become lifetime fans who will read your blog posts and share them.

Look for coupon codes: People love freebies; your audience is not exempted! If you can get discount/coupon codes to some websites that allow affiliates, you can bet that you will have many people streaming to buy the product before the discount period runs out. Simply look for a product that your audience would love to have, have your affiliate link and then get a coupon code that they can key in at checkout; they will thank you and you will earn some money in the process.

And if you don't want to promote other people's products only for you to take portion of the selling price, you could instead develop your own products for sale. Let's discuss how to go about it next.

Make Passive Income By Creating Your Own Product and Selling It Online

As I have insisted since the beginning, if you want to make passive income, you MUST invest something; it could be your time, money or other resources. Instead of making money for other people when you don't have control over the products that you are promoting, you can develop your own products then sell them online (you can recruit affiliates to market it for you!). The good thing about selling downloadable digital products online is that once a product becomes popular, you can be sure of making unimaginable amounts of passive income without doing much to maintain it since everything can be automated.

Such products could be:

- Music

- Software

- Plugins

- Themes

- Mobile apps

- Photos

- Designs and patterns

- Courses

- Fonts and vector images

- Etc.

Obviously, for this to work, you need to invest time, money, skill and other resources to develop the product and to market it to the target audience.

So how exactly should you go about it? Here are some general steps to follow:

Step 1: Decide on a niche

The thing is; the number of options as far as the products you can develop is unlimited. That's why you have to choose the niche that you want to focus on otherwise you will find yourself feeling overwhelmed at the thought of 'what digital product can I sell online?'

The best strategy to follow when choosing a niche is to determine what you are most interested in, your current skills level, your current problems etc. If you experience certain problems, there is likely to be millions of others out there who may have faced such problems.

You can develop a digital product to solve your problem. This route is likely to be the easiest for many beginners because by developing a product that solves your problems, this means you will be the product's first user so you can critic it, know its strengths, and analyze it at a deeper level to ensure it serves the purpose you want it to serve.

Note: Your digital product does not always have to solve a problem. You can develop a digital product that's in line with your passions. For instance, if you are passionate about photography, you can package your photos then sell them on different stock photography sites. And if you love singing but never got a chance to record your music for whatever reason, you can record your music then sell online e.g. on iTunes, and Tunecore.

Step 2: Determine the nature of product

After identifying a niche, the next step is to decide the nature of product that solves the problem or fulfils the purpose for which you want the product to serve. For instance, if you are a social media manager who has been frustrated with the idea of not being able to manage customer accounts in one central location or not being able to know when your customer's name is mentioned online, this means you need a product that will help you to solve the problem. Based on the nature of the problem, the best product to solve the problem could be a cloud based tool, software or mobile app. The approach you take when deciding whether to publish a book, develop a course, develop a plugin etc. is likely to be different. For instance, if you want to publish a book, you may for instance use your knowledge and experience in a certain field, as the first step in deciding a niche (the niche in this case is what you want to teach others). If you know something very well and have been getting questions from people, you could for instance develop a course, which answers the questions you have been answering people repeatedly.

The most important thing is to first identify the problem then think of the best way to solve the problem. Once you have an idea of what you want to develop, you need to ask yourself one important question:

Step 3: Do you have the skills?

The next step is to analyze your current skills and decide on the approach you want to take to develop the product. Do you have the skill needed to develop the product? If you do have the skill, then go ahead and develop the product. But if you don't have the skill, don't worry; you can outsource much of the work to other people who can do it for you at a very affordable price. The top places you can find people to outsource to include: Upwork.com, Fiverr.com, Guru.com and Freelancer.com. On these platforms, you will find people who have all manner of skills including programming, graphics design, video and photo editing, ghostwriting, editing, translation, web development, mobile app development etc.; the options are limitless!

All you need to do is to give the contractor instructions on what it is that you want to create, keep the communications lines open and sit back to wait for the job to be done. It is recommended that you see milestones of what it is the contractor is doing to ensure he/she is doing work that meets your expectations.

Step 4: What to do once the product is ready

Once the product is ready, the next step is to package it, list it for sale then market it extensively. Let's briefly discuss each of these:

Package your product

Different digital products call for different forms of packaging just before sale. For instance, if you are selling ebooks, you should invest a lot in a good cover as well as proper formatting of the book to ensure it wows your readership from the moment they see it. Good copyrighting does an amazing job of bringing out the level of value that a user/customer will derive from using the product. Therefore, you shouldn't skimp on that. Prepare the product to be in a format that makes it easy for the customer to derive the expected value. For instance, if your product is software, you need to make sure that it is in a format that the reader can easily open without needing any other additional tools/software. It should also be easy for use across different operating systems if you really want to attract a large user base. Therefore, whatever you do, make sure that the landing page has great copyrighting, has testimonials and gives prospective customers the confidence that they will derive the expected value.

List for sale

The nature of the product will greatly influence where you list it. For instance, yours is a mobile app, Google Play Store and Apple Store would be the places where your target audience is expected to get the app from so if possible, make sure to have the app available for use on all devices and operating systems. If yours is a book, you may want to list it on your blog (If you have any) and if you want to leverage on the popularity of other platforms, then selling the book on a platform like Amazon Kindle Direct Publishing is perhaps the one place you can be sure to attract sales within a very short period. For WordPress themes, you sell them on your website, list them on WordPress website or on marketplaces like ThemeForest. And if you have software, you could list it on places like E-junkie.com, Sellfy.com, FastSpring.com, Shopify.com, PayLoadz.com, ClickBank.com, Amazon.com etc. If you have knitting designs and patterns for instance, you can sell them on your online store, Shopify or on Etsy. If you are selling a course, you can sell it on your online store, Udemy.com, Teachable.com and other similar sites.

Many of the above websites have systems that are easy to follow so the chance of making a mistake when preparing your product for sale is likely to be low.

Once your product is live, the next step is to market/promote it.

Market and promote

Marketing and promoting your product is perhaps the one thing that will determine the success or failure of your product. You really shouldn't expect the product to 'sell itself' after you've published it. Even if you already had an audience that you promote to e.g. a mailing list or a blog audience, you need to be proactive in promoting the product if you want to make worthwhile income.

Some of the ways to make consistent income from your product include:

✓ Having people leave positive reviews about the product (on the market place and on blog posts)

✓ Giving freebies or discounts for the product then asking for review

✓ Working with affiliates

✓ Promoting the product on social networks and different online forums etc.

If you have a great product, you definitely need to start working with affiliates because if you have good payouts along with good reviews, the chances that you will attract tens or even hundreds of affiliates who will be promoting your product are high. This will definitely help you to literally make money on autopilot. You can list your product on popular affiliate websites like JVZoo.com, CJ.com, Shareasale.com, ClickBank.com etc.

Make Passive Income with YouTube

Did you know that YouTube gets about a billion new users each month? With such an audience, you would understand why YouTube is among the top rated platforms to generate passive income today. Just to put this into perspective, with each 1,000 views on your video, you get a return of $2-$4. While this might not seem like much, just consider making a hundred videos that have 5,000 views each. I'll leave the math to you.

What's more, the entire process is very simple - you only have to follow the steps below:

1. **Create a YouTube channel**

2. **Pick a suitable niche**

First, consider that while there are many niches out there, only four really matter today if you ask me. These include happiness, love, health and wealth.

3. **Pick a good strategy**

The second thing you have to note is that you need to look for an easy way to make this work- this includes modelling what already works.

Go to the YouTube search bar and search a common question related to the above niches. You'll get recommended searches. That right there is YouTube telling you what people want- because that's what people are searching for. The only thing you have to do now is create content around that. When you become persistent in creating videos based on the recommendations, you start getting consistent traffic and in no time, YouTube will start recommending you!

After that, go to the top channels in your niche. You want to find top You Tubers talking about the same topics you are talking about. Go to their channels and begin sorting by the phrases 'most popular'. By doing so, you'll get all the videos giving these content creators the millions of views. With that, you'll have enough info to able to create your own video a few minutes later and upload it.

Monetizing

So how do you make money from all these views (which I'm sure you'll be getting in no time)?

Step 1

Log in to your channel account. Go to the channels settings tab and click "enable monetization." Accept the monetization agreement by following the steps indicated.

Next, go to the 'uploads' tab; there, you will be able to see a green box that has a dollar sign right beside the videos that are eligible for monetization.

Step 2

You'll now have to link your AdSense account to your channel. In case you don't have one, note that it's free to create an AdSense account. You'll only require a mailing address, bank account or PayPal for your account to be verified.

YouTube will then place ads in your videos and you'll start earning from revenues generated by these ads. You also have to note that you'll earn based on the type of ads displayed and the pricing of the ads. The ads which will be appearing in the beginning of your video (pre-roll ads) usually generate more money for every 1000 views than the banners that are generally less obtrusive.

Make Passive Income With Membership Site

A membership site is simply what it is; a membership site. People pay to be allowed to access content that is only available for members. You can create a membership area within your WordPress site using a plugin such as MemberPress or S2member.

So what is it that you can limit access to? Well, you can have a course where you teach your members something that you know best, have value added products, offer bundles/packages to books and other content that would make sense to pay for access etc. You can even have webinars, podcasts, ebooks and other types of content within the members area. So how exactly can you get started with a membership site? Let's discuss that next.

How to Get Started With Membership Sites

To start your membership site:

Step 1: Create a Membership Site (With WordPress)

From the above discussion, you already know how to create a website using WordPress. You will need this knowledge to create a membership site. WordPress is the best platform since it takes care of all back end stuff required to run a membership site.

Using WordPress, go to plugins, search for S2member plugin, and install it. Make sure to fill all fields such the price for your services and products and the payment details (on PayPal button) to ensure the visitors get the information they need to know before they subscribe.

Your visitors will join or subscribe to your membership site and make payments through the PayPal button to get a username and password (from you) which will help them access the member's area that has your products or services.

Remember to set up your membership site. This means you will have to fill "general option" tab and fill out all the fields to ensure your membership site is functioning well.

Membership sites often have membership levels with level 1 being the lowest and level 4 the highest. You need to set this up by selecting the level you want to restrict to paying members only and which level to designate to each post.

Step 2: Building a Membership Base

It might be difficult to get people willing to pay a fee for your site every month, but with the help of the following tips, you will build a strong membership site.

Build trust: To gain trust, you can offer a free trial. People like trying things out before purchasing them. When you use this method, you will increase your sign up rate and since you offer good products and services, you will get more members compared to if you did not have a free trial.

You can also decide to offer a free level of membership. Leaving one level free and charging the rest will also get you more members and within no time, the amount of money your site generates in a month will surprise you. You can use Wishlist Member plugin to offer some freebies.

You can also build trust by building your membership base on a separate site using the same niche (your blog is good enough if you are serious about it). Building a free membership base and letting people use it will earn you trust and loyalty and every time you launch a new membership site using the same niche, you will have many subscribers.

Step 3: Drive Traffic to Your New Membership Site

You have to increase traffic to your blog by growing the list of loyal audience and raving fans. How can you do that? The first thing you need to do is to create a highly converting lead magnet. Some people call it bribes, content upgrades, freebies, or signup incentives.

A lead magnet is an irresistible 'bribe' where you can decide to offer a valuable service or content such as a 5 minutes free consultation, a free PDF checklist, a video, or eBook to your target audience in exchange for their contact information.

Whichever method or route you decide to use, make sure it is appealing to your target audience and it solves a common problem for your target audience. This will help you create a long-term audience relationship.

You can also drive traffic to your membership site by reaching out to influential bloggers. Instead of posting your content on social media and waiting for an influencer to notice it, directly pitch your content. If your content is valuable, influencers will share it with their social media followers. Do not just send your content to influential bloggers and wait for them to share it for you. Everybody it doing that, you need a better plan such as this one:

Choose your hit list: Identify about 20 influential bloggers who actively engage their/your target audience, accepts guest posts, and have some social authority.

Let them notice you: Subscribe or join their group. Read, comment, and share their blogs as many times as possible; this will ensure they notice you. It may take a couple of weeks to happen, but eventually, someone will take note. In addition, send them complimentary emails. It might sound like a lot of work, but the rewards are astonishing.

Send them a pitch email: Send them a quick, on point email asking them to check out your content. If your content is good, they will surely share it because you have already built a strong relationship with them.

Step 4: Keep Your Members Happy

If you want to keep your passive income flowing, keep its source (your members) happy. Do not give them a reason to unsubscribe from your site. To avoid this, provide your members with fresh, up to date, and valuable information.

Create different types of membership sites using software subscriber (the best license software where you pay a monthly or yearly fee to access your membership site). Some of the ideas you can post on your new membership sites are mentor blogs, offer services such as Forex tips, stocks, or sports betting tips, content addressing adults, or the community. Just remember to keep updating your membership site.

Step 5: Delegate Tasks

Having established different membership sites that generate a passive income, you can delegate some daily activities to get more time to think of new and good content you can use to create more and more sites.

Hire people to write your content (after you have drafted it) and let them respond to members' comments and requests. By doing so, you will have a chance to expand your income streams and drive them to a point where they can earn you thousands of dollars every day.

Strategies For Making Money From Your Membership Site

The prospect of starting your own membership site, and hoping to make a profit from it, may seem quite daunting. However, the secret here, as is the case in most internet businesses, is to actually go ahead and do something. You just need to make sure your approach is smart; this will give you a leg up over your opposition.

Here are a few things you need to do to optimize your chances of succeeding at running a membership site.

1: Start right now, especially if you think you are not ready

Do you think you are not good enough? Do you think you still do not have a good enough product to offer? Well, you will never be completely ready, so you may as well start right now.

If you are not sure if you have sufficient material to offer, try doing any of the following:

Begin with a ridiculously low fee. Use your charter members as your guinea pigs and encourage them to give you constant feedback.

Aim for a Minimum Viable Product (MVP) rather than absolute perfection. Your membership site does not have to be a fierce competitor to "Teaching Sells."

2: Learn from the membership sites you patronize

Do you belong to a specific membership site? Look at their structure and see if you can take something from it. For instance, you can take the following ideas and implement them into your own thing:

Monthly seminars with the occasional guest speaker

Monthly calls that involve Q&A

Forums for members

A private Facebook group for members

If you are in a membership site you feel could be better, examine those areas you would improve if you were running it, and apply what you find in your own site.

3: Constantly interact & engage with the members of your site

You could begin a membership site that is simply a dripped content feed with little or no input from your part, and this is fine since many membership sites are like that. However, understand that members will have a much stronger reason to join your site if they know they have insider access to you.

Depending on how you set up your site, you could:

Set up live seminars or even webinars where members can ask questions

Forums where you get to post regularly, providing tips and aid for your members

A text chat room where you hold office hours or a similar thing.

Make Passive Income With Peer-2-Peer lending

If you have some extra cash to spare, you can lend it to someone who is in need through various peer-peer lending platforms online. These platforms act like a marketplace where investors (who have money) get to meet borrowers (those who are looking for money) in an organized manner. The platforms weed out the bad guys and facilitate the process to ensure transparency as well as minimize the risk of loss. In the process, you earn a tidy interest (more than what you can earn from your bank) while the borrower gets to pay lower interest than he/she would otherwise have paid had he/shed borrowed directly from a bank. That's not all; loans are processed a lot faster. Some of the top P2P lending platforms include the following:

- The Lending Club

- Funding circle

- Zopa

- Prosper

- Ratesetter

- Lendinvest

With these sites, you can earn anywhere between 7-8% return.

Bonus: Diversify Your Passive Income By Investing In Stocks

I have come to realize that stocks paying dividends regularly are usually stable businesses much like the retail REITs as they have shown the ability to be a bit less delicate to market cycles.

While dividend income takes quite some time to create, you can still build a good income that pays on a regular basis over time, if you are a disciplined and prudent investor.

For instance, if you invest $1000, and your dividend yield is 4%, you will be having $4000 income every year, and when you compound the dividend payments, the returns become even higher.

The reason I chose to include stock investing in this book is that stocks have done better than bonds, real estate and CDs, which makes them a worthy venture. Therefore, if you want a piece of this cake, pool some cash, do a little bit of research and begin investing. You however need to bear in mind that you need to start small and educate yourself along the way if you are new to this because with the potential for profit comes a higher risk of losing cash.

NOTE: As many experts would advise, don't expect to get the most from the stock market if you don't have a plan to avoid touching the investment for about five or ten years. Nonetheless, others argue that targeting daily or hourly fluctuations in the market is better. Therefore, you need to make a decision here- based on your preference and overall investment strategy.

How to invest in stocks online

With technology, things are amazingly simple; there are sites tailored for you such as Ameritrade and E-Trade that are readily available for you to start investing in stocks online. The two are currently some of the most popular electronic brokerages even though most big firms also have online options as well.

When you open an account with any of these brokerages (such as Ameritrade), you inform your broker the number of stocks, and types you want to buy. The broker makes the trade on your behalf for a commission (this is usually a couple cents per share). By going online, you stand at an advantage because online trading sites will always charge lower commissions because anyway, the trading is done electronically.

Once you select the stocks you want to buy, you have the option of making a 'limit order' or a 'market order'. When you ask for a stock purchase at the prevailing price in the market, we call that a 'market order'. On the other hand, a limit order is when you ask to purchase a stock at a limited price. Let's look at an example;

You want to purchase some stocks in Dell, which at present are trading at $80 for say, $70. The broker in this case could wait to obtain the shares until the price has met your limit.

Purchasing stocks through brokers definitely has its advantages but there are other ways as well that you could consider when buying stocks. You can for instance buy stocks through the company directly. Sites such as DRIPInvestor.com provide lists of companies that accept direct purchasing of stocks.

I need your help...

We have come to the end of the book. Thank you for reading and congratulations for reading until the end.

The above are not all the ways through which you can generate passive income online. Nonetheless, I believe all this information will help you to get started. Start your passive income project today. Do whatever it takes to develop and establish it, and wait for your reward (the great positive change in your financial status)

Finally, if you enjoyed this book, then I'd like to ask you for a favor, would you be kind enough to leave a review for this book on Amazon? It'd be greatly appreciated!

I want to reach as many people as I can with this book, and more reviews will help me accomplish that!

If you have any questions or problems, please contact us: hello@freedomdestination.com

Thank you and good luck!

Preview Of '20 Easy And Fast Diet Tips For Losing Weight'

Before we start learning about the strategies you can use to lose weight, let's start by highlighting some of the benefits that will come as a result of shedding those extra pounds just to give you extra motivation to want to do something NOW.

Why You Need To Lose Weight

Healthy weight loss has over one hundred benefits; these include emotional and physical benefits. I will dedicate this section to discussing the health benefits that many people (and weight loss/health books) do not pay enough attention to.

1: You Avoid Pre-Diabetes or Type 2 Diabetes

Pre-diabetes/high blood glucose is a condition that develops when the blood sugar levels in your blood move past normal ranges but not enough to qualify as diabetes. When your body stops consistently producing insulin sufficient to meet your body's needs, or the amount produced does not work properly, type 2 diabetes is likely to develop. Being pre-diabetic places you at a very high risk of developing type 2 diabetes.

Being obese or overweight is a proven leading risk factor for type 2 diabetes because carrying excess weight typically makes it hard for cells to respond to insulin, and since the additional fat acts as an insulating layer, it makes it more difficult for the sugar to enter the cells, which results in more circulating blood sugar levels.

Nonetheless, if you are already a pre-diabetic, you can prevent the progression to diabetes by shedding some weight (to reduce the insulating layer on cells so that they respond more to insulin) and trying to maintain a healthy weight.

2: You Keep Your Heart Healthy

When it comes to heart disease, some of the key risk factors are high cholesterol and high blood pressure. Research shows that:

1. Excessive accumulation of body fat makes your body release particular chemicals that occur naturally into the bloodstream, which increases blood pressure, and

2. Being overweight makes the liver produce too much amounts of Low density Lipoprotein (LDL) also called cholesterol. LDL tends to be sticky and gathers in the walls of blood vessels, which causes the narrowing of arteries, a condition called atherosclerosis, which increases your risk of strokes and heart attack.

When you lose weight, your blood pressure often reduces and the liver naturally reduces the amount of LDL it produces.

Royal Adelaide Hospital conducted a research on cardiovascular improvements with respect to a special weight loss program. Their results showed a decrease of cholesterol by 12%, a 10% decrease of LDL, a 5% decrease in diastolic blood pressure, and an 8% decrease in systolic blood pressure.

3: Improved Sleep (and Possible Treatment of Sleep Apnea)

One of the most prominent benefits of losing weight is improved sleep. When you gain excess weight, you gather more soft tissues in the neck; this intensifies the incidence of snoring.

NOTE: Snoring is a result of constricted airways, which obstructs air movement.

Snoring can be a symptom of sleep apnea, a possible life-threatening condition characterized by obstruction of breathing that requires the victim to wake up frequently from sleep to resume breathing.

As a victim of sleep apnea, you rarely remember anything about the episodes of waking many times a night to breathe but even so, this sleep and oxygen deprivation could easily lead to a weak immune system, high blood pressure, heart disease, memory problems, and sexual dysfunction.

When you lose weight, you reduce the amount of fatty tissue in the back of your throat, decrease snoring and the likelihood of the worsening of your health- as aforementioned. You encourage better sleep quality and reduce the risk of developing sleep apnea.

4: Better Joints (Mobile and Pain-Free)

Osteoarthritis (OA) is one of the most common joint disorders. It causes the tissues that protect the joints (cartilage and bone) to wear away. Consequently, the joints become tender and swollen, thus making movement very painful.

When you are overweight, you add to the load placed on the joints that bear the weight such as hips and knees.

NOTE: When you walk, you exert a force of approximately 3-6 times your entire body weight across the knee (read more on this page (check the discussion section) or here), so adding about 10 kg of weight does increase the force on the knees, which is equal to carrying 30-60 kgs^2 extra.

Therefore, a loss of merely 5% of your body weight could reduce the amount of stress placed on the knees, lower back, and hips, and reduce the pain (remember that losing 5kgs is equal to relieving a force of 15-30kgs^2 on the knees). According to doctors, a 10% loss of bodyweight has presented a 28% improvement in knee osteoarthritis symptoms.

Check out the rest of 20 Easy And Fast Diet Tips For Losing Weight on Amazon, go to: http://amzn.to/2mNtPEg

Check Out My Other Books

Below you'll find some of my other popular books that are popular on Amazon and Kindle as well

Alternatively, you can visit my author page on Amazon to see other work done by me.

Ketogenic Cookbook: Quick Low Calorie Ketogenic Crockpot Recipes with 7 Days Meal Plan

Freedom: How to Make Money Online and Become Financially Free by Creating Passive Income

Mediterranean Diet: Instant Pot Cookbook with Delicious Recipes

Alice the Superbug

Madison and Astrid's first magical journey

Intermittent Fasting: The Essential Beginners Guide for Women for Weight Loss

Chakra Healing: Chakra Healing and Karmic Awareness for Beginners

SEO 2017 for Growth: The Ultimate Guide to Learn Search Engine Optimization with Internet Marketing Tips

Psychology: How to Analyze People Using Human Psychological Techniques, Body Language Signals, Social Skills and Personality Types

Paleo Smoothies: Recipes to Energize and for Ultimate Health and Weight Loss

Belly Diet Smoothies: Delicious Smoothie Recipes to Flatten Your Belly, Improve Your Gut & Burn Fat

Keto Diet: Keto Diet Guide Cookbook for Beginners with Meal Plan and Simple, Delicious Recipes to Lose Weight and Look Good

Online Business from Scratch: The 9 Step Guide to Building a Profitable and Sustainable Online Business

Weight Loss: 20 Easy And Fast Diet Tips For Losing Weight - An Easy-To-Follow Weight Loss Guide

Ketogenic Cookbook: Ketogenic Cookbook for Beginners with 7 Days Meal Plan

Negative Calorie Diet: Cookbook & Guide Which Will Help You To Burn Body Fat, Lose Weight And Live Healthy

Negative Calorie Diet with Anti-Inflammatory Diet Guide

Make Money Online To Achieve Freedom

Negative Calorie Diet with Smart Fat Guide

Negative Calorie Diet & Clean Eating: Cookbook & Guide Which Will Help You To Burn Body Fat, Lose Weight And Live Healthy

Smart Fat: Cookbook with Fat Meals Which Help You to Lose Weight, Get Healthy and Improve Brain Function

Anti-Inflammatory Diet Guide: The Guide to Reduce Inflammation and Live a Healthy Life Without Pain

Essential Oils: The Young Living Book Guide of Natural Remedies for Beginners for Pets, For Dogs

Clean Eating: Cookbook and Guide to Restore Your Body's Natural Balance and Eat Healthy

Anti-Inflammatory Diet Guide: The Guide to Reduce Inflammation and Live a Healthy Life Without Pain

Dash Diet: Cookbook for Weight Loss with Action Plan and Easy Recipes

Air Fryer Cookbook: Quick, Healthy and Easy Low Carb Air Fryer Recipes

Psychology & Habits Of Highly Effective People Box Set

Leptin Resistance: Leptin Diet to Control Your Hormones, Get Permanent Weight Loss, Cure Obesity and Live Healthy

Negative Calorie Diet & Dash Diet Box Set

Negative Calorie Diet & Weight Loss Box Set

Habits of Highly Effective People: What Are the Habits of Successful People?

Slow Cooker: Cookbook with Slow Cooker Recipes

Weight Loss Cookbook: Meal Prep Cookbook for Weight Loss and Clean Eating

Weight Loss Cookbook: Mediterranean Diet for Lasting Weight Loss

Negative Calorie Diet & Dash Diet Box Set

Slow Cooker & Instant Pot Box Set

Children Books: Madison and Astrid's first magical journey & Alice the Superbug Box Set

Belly Diet: The Zero Belly Diet Step-By-Step Guide Which Helps You to Lose Your Belly and Enjoy Your Flat Belly

Weight Loss: 20 Easy and Fast Diet Tips for Losing Weight - An Easy-To-Follow Weight Loss Guide

Instant Pot: Instant Pot Pressure Cooker Cookbook with Easy and Healthy Recipes

Vegan Cookbook: Vegan Cookbook For Beginners, For Kids And For Teens For Diabetics With Pictures

Low Carb: Low Carb Diet Cookbook with Low Carb Keto Recipes for Batch Cooking

Ketogenic Cooking: Ketogenic Cooking With Your Instant Pot

Passive Income: Passive Income Tutorial with 7 Online Ideas to Generate Passive Income Streams for Beginners

Low Carb Diet: Low Carb Diet Recipes Cookbook for Beginners for Batch Cooking

Make Money from Home: How to Make Money Online and Escape the 9-5 Rat Race

Amazon Customer Service

Kindle Unlimited

Bonus: Subscribe To The Free Enhance Your Business Report!

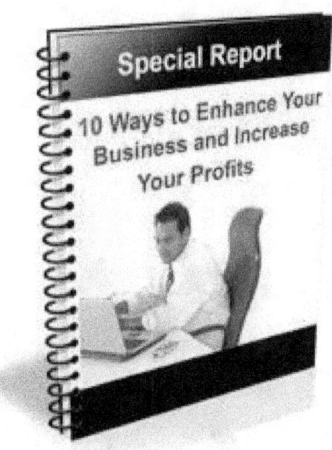

When you subscribe to Freedom Destination via email, you will get free access to a report. All you have to do is enter your email address to get instant access.

This report is going to discuss 10 important, and possible crucial facts/ideas that if implemented, will increase your business as well as your profits.

Or you can access it here: http://bit.ly/2tXwgKQ